QUINTET

tap tap tap tap tap

tap tap tap tap tap

6017

4

FROM THE ART OF FUGUE
CONTRAPUNCTUS V

(1685-1750)
JOHANN SEBASTIAN BACH
Edited by Robert King

RICERCAR DEL PRIMO TUONO

PALESTRINA
(1525-1594)
Edited by Robert King

TWO PIECES

From Neue Ausserlesene Paduanen, Galliarden, Cantzonen,
Almand und Coranten (Hamburg, 1609)

ALMAND

WILLIAM BRADE

Edited by Robert King

6017

TWO PAVANS

From Newer Paven, Galliarden, und Intraden (Coburgk, 1603)

MELCHIOR FRANCK
Edited by Robert King

FROM THE ART OF FUGUE
CONTRAPUNCTUS 1

JOHANN SEBASTIAN BACH
(1685-1750)

Edited by Robert King

11

SONATA NO. 25

FROM HORA DECIMA (LEIPZIG, 1670)

JOHANN PEZEL
(1639-1694)
Edited by Robert King

OVERTURE TO BERENICE
TRANSCRIBED BY EDWIN GLICK

GEORG FREDERIC HANDEL

VOLUNTARY ON OLD 100TH
TRANSCRIBED BY JOHN CORLEY

TROMBONE

HENRY PURCELL
(1658-1695)

Music Minus One CLARINET Compact Discs

___ MMO CD 3201 Mozart Clarinet Concerto in A major
___ MMO CD 3202 Weber Clarinet Concerto No. 1 in F minor, Op. 73
　　　　　　　　 Stamitz Clarinet Concerto No. 3 in Bb major
___ MMO CD 3203 Spohr Clarinet Concerto No. 1 in C minor, Op. 26
___ MMO CD 3204 Weber Clarinet Concertino, Opus 26
___ MMO CD 3205 First Chair Clarinet Solos *Orchestral Excerpts*
___ MMO CD 3206 The Art Of The Solo Clarinet *Orchestral Excerpts*
___ MMO CD 3207 Mozart: Quintet for Clarinet and Strings in A, K.581
___ MMO CD 3208 Brahms: Sonatas Opus 120, Nos. 1 & 2
___ MMO CD 3209 Weber: Grand Duo Concertant - Wagner: Adagio
___ MMO CD 3210 Schumann Fantasy Pieces, Opus 73, Three Romances
___ MMO CD 3211 Easy Clarinet Solos, Student Editions 1-3 years
___ MMO CD 3212 Easy Clarinet Solos, Student Editions 1-3 years, vol. 2
___ MMO CD 3213 Easy Jazz Duets, Student Editions, 1-3 years

Choice selections for the Clarinet, drawn from the very best solo literature for the instrument. The pieces are performed by the foremost virtuosi of our time, artists affiliated with the New York Philharmonic, Boston, Chicago, Cleveland and Philadelphia Orchestras, The Juilliard School, Curtis Institute of Music, Indiana University and the Univerity of Toronto, as well as the Metropolitan Opera Orchestra.

The repertoire and editions used in the Laureate Series correspond to the approved music lists of various Music Education Associations and may be performed as contest solos in State Music Festivals. Contest regulations, such as time limitations have been taken into consideration.

Beginning	Intermediate	Advanced	Level
___ MMO CD 3221	Jerome Bunke, Clinician		B
___ MMO CD 3222	Harold Wright, Boston Symphony		B
___ MMO CD 3223	Stanley Drucker, N.Y. Philharmonic		I
___ MMO CD 3224	Jerome Bunke, Clinician		I
___ MMO CD 3225	Stanley Drucker, N.Y. Philharmonic		A
___ MMO CD 3226	Harold Wright, Boston Symphony		A
___ MMO CD 3227	Stanley Drucker, N.Y. Philharmonic		I
___ MMO CD 3228	Stanley Drucker, N.Y. Philharmonic		A
___ MMO CD 3229	Harold Wright, Boston Symphony		A

Music Minus One TROMBONE Compact Discs

___ MMO CD 3901 Easy Solos, Student Editions, Beginning Level vol. 1
___ MMO CD 3902 Easy Solos, Student Editions, Beginning Level vol. 2
___ MMO CD 3903 Easy Jazz Duets, Student Editions, 1-3 years

Choice selections for the Trombone, drawn from the very best solo literature for the instrument. The pieces are performed by the foremost virtuosi of our time, artists affiliated with the New York Philharmonic, Boston, Chicago, Cleveland and Philadelphia Orchestras, The Juilliard School, Curtis Institute of Music, Indiana University and the Univerity of Toronto, as well as the Metropolitan Opera Orchestra.

The repertoire and editions used in the Laureate Series correspond to the approved music lists of various Music Education Associations and may be performed as contest solos in State Music Festivals. Contest regulations, such as time limitations have been taken into consideration.

Beginning	Intermediate	Advanced	Level
___ MMO CD 3911	Per Brevig, Metropolitan Opera Orch.		B
___ MMO CD 3912	Jay Friedman, Chicago Symphony		B
___ MMO CD 3913	Keith Brown, Soloist, Prof. Indiana Univ.		I
___ MMO CD 3914	Jay Friedman, Chicago Symphony		I
___ MMO CD 3915	Keith Brown, Soloist, Prof. Indiana Univ.		A
___ MMO CD 3916	Per Brevig, Metropolitan Opera Orch.		A
___ MMO CD 3917	Keith Brown, Soloist, Prof. Indiana Univ.		A
___ MMO CD 3918	Jay Friedman, Chicago Symphony		A
___ MMO CD 3919	Per Brevig, Metropolitan Opera Orch.		A

Music Minus One ALTO SAX Compact Discs

___ MMO CD 4101 Easy Solos, Student Editions, Beginning Level vol. 1
___ MMO CD 4102 Easy Solos, Student Editions, Beginning Level vol. 2
___ MMO CD 4103 Easy Jazz Duets, Student Editions, 1-3 years
___ MMO CD 4104 For Saxes Only, Arr. by Bob Wilber

Choice selections for the Alto Sax, drawn from the very best solo literature for the instrument. The pieces are performed by the foremost virtuosi of our time, artists affiliated with the New York Philharmonic, Boston, Chicago, Cleveland and Philadelphia Orchestras, The Juilliard School, Curtis Institute of Music, Indiana University and the Univerity of Toronto, as well as the Metropolitan Opera Orchestra.

Beginning	Intermediate	Advanced	Level
___ MMO CD 4111	Paul Brodie, Canadian Soloist		B
___ MMO CD 4112	Vincent Abato, Metropolitan Opera Orch.		B
___ MMO CD 4113	Paul Brodie, Canadian Soloist		I
___ MMO CD 4114	Vincent Abato, Metropolitan Opera Orch.		I
___ MMO CD 4115	Paul Brodie, Canadian Soloist, Clinician		A
___ MMO CD 4116	Vincent Abato, Metropolitan Opera Orch.		A
___ MMO CD 4117	Paul Brodie, Canadian Soloist, Clinician		A
___ MMO CD 4118	Vincent Abato, Metropolitan Opera Orch.		A

The repertoire and editions used in the Laureate Series correspond to the approved music lists of various Music Education Associations and may be performed as contest solos in State Music Festivals. Contest regulations, such as time limitations have been taken into consideration.

Music Minus One OBOE Compact Discs

___ MMO CD 3400 Albinoni Three Oboe Concerti Opus 7 No. 3, No. 6, Opus 9 No. 2
___ MMO CD 3401 3 Oboe Concerti: Handel, Telemann, Vivaldi
___ MMO CD 3402 Mozart/Stamitz Oboe Quartets in F major (K.370; Op.8 #3)

Music Minus One TRUMPET Compact Discs

___ MMO CD 3801 3 Trumpet Concerti Handel/Telemann/Vivaldi
___ MMO CD 3802 Easy Solos, Student Edition, Beginning Level vol. 1
___ MMO CD 3803 Easy Solos, Student Edition, Beginning Level vol. 2
___ MMO CD 3804 Easy Jazz Duets with Rhythm Section, Beginning Level
___ MMO CD 3805 Music for Brass Ensemble

Choice selections for the Trumpet, drawn from the very best solo literature for the instrument. The pieces are performed by the foremost virtuosi of our time, artists affiliated with the New York Philharmonic, Boston, Chicago, Cleveland and Philadelphia Orchestras, The Juilliard School, Curtis Institute of Music, Indiana University and the Univerity of Toronto, as well as the Metropolitan Opera Orchestra.

Beginning	Intermediate	Advanced	Level
___ MMO CD 3811	Gerard Schwarz, N.Y. Philharmonic		B
___ MMO CD 3812	Armando Ghitalia, Boston Symphony		B
___ MMO CD 3813	Robert Nagel, Soloist, NY Brass Ensemble		I
___ MMO CD 3814	Gerard Schwarz, N.Y. Philharmonic		I
___ MMO CD 3815	Robert Nagel, Soloist NY Brass Ensemble		A
___ MMO CD 3816	Armando Ghitalia, Boston Symphony		I
___ MMO CD 3817	Gerard Schwarz, N.Y. Philharmonic		I
___ MMO CD 3818	Robert Nagel, Soloist, NY Brass Ensemble		A
___ MMO CD 3819	Armando Ghitalia, Boston Symphony		A
___ MMO CD 3820	Raymond Crisara, Concert Soloist		B
___ MMO CD 3821	Raymond Crisara, Concert Soloist		B
___ MMO CD 3822	Raymond Crisara, Concert Soloist		I

The repertoire and editions used in the Laureate Series correspond to the approved music lists of various Music Education Associations and may be performed as contest solos in State Music Festivals. Contest regulations, such as time limitations have been taken into consideration.

Music Minus One DRUMMER Compact Discs

___ MMO CD 5001 MODERN JAZZ DRUMMING, 2 CD Set
___ MMO CD 5002 FOR DRUMMERS ONLY!
___ MMO CD 5003 WIPE-OUT!
___ MMO CD 5004 SIT IN!
___ *MMO CD 5005 DRUM STAR
___ *MMO CD 5006 DRUMPADSTICKSKIN
___ *MMO CD 5007 LIGHT MY FIRE
___ *MMO CD 5008 FIRE AND RAIN
___ *MMO CD 5009 CLASSICAL PERCUSSION, 2 CD Set
*Winter '95/Spring '96 Release

Music Minus One BROADWAY Shows

___ MMO CD 1016 Les Mis/Phantom
___ MMO CD 1067 Guys And Dolls
___ MMO CD 1100 West Side Story
　　　　　　　　 2 CDs
___ MMO CD 1110 Cabaret
___ MMO CD 1173 Camelot
___ MMO CD 1174 My Fair Lady
　　　　　　　　 2 CDs
___ MMO CD 1175 Oklahoma
___ MMO CD 1176 The Sound Of Music
　　　　　　　　 2 CDs
___ MMO CD 1177 South Pacific
___ MMO CD 1178 The King And I
　　　　　　　　 2 CDs
___ MMO CD 1179 Fiddler On The Roof
___ MMO CD 1180 Carousel
___ MMO CD 1181 Porgy And Bess
___ MMO CD 1183 The Music Man
___ MMO CD 1184 Showboat
___ MMO CD 1186 Annie Get Your Gun
　　　　　　　　 2 CDs
___ MMO CD 1187 Hello Dolly
　　　　　　　　 2 CDs
___ MMO CD 1189 Oliver

Music Minus One PIANO Compact Discs

___ MMO CD 3001 Beethoven Piano Concerto No. 1 in C, Opus 15
___ MMO CD 3002 Beethoven Piano Concerto No. 2 in Bb, Opus 19
___ MMO CD 3003 Beethoven Piano Concerto No. 3 in Cm, Opus 37
___ MMO CD 3004 Beethoven Piano Concerto No. 4 in G, Opus 58
___ MMO CD 3005 Beethoven Piano Concerto No. 5 in Eb, Opus 73
___ MMO CD 3006 Grieg Piano Concerto in A minor, Opus 16
___ MMO CD 3007 Rachmaninoff Piano Concerto No. 2 in C minor
___ MMO CD 3008 Schumann Piano Concerto in A minor, Opus 54
___ MMO CD 3009 Brahms Piano Concerto No. 1 in D minor, Opus 15
___ MMO CD 3010 Chopin Piano Concerto No. 1 in Em, Opus 11
___ MMO CD 3011 Mendelssohn Piano Concerto No. 1 in Gm, Opus 25
___ MMO CD 3012 W.A. Mozart Piano Concerto No. 9 in Ebm, K.271
___ MMO CD 3013 W.A. Mozart Piano Concerto No. 12 in A, K.414
___ MMO CD 3014 W.A. Mozart Piano Concerto No. 20 in Dm, K.466
___ MMO CD 3015 W.A. Mozart Piano Concerto No. 23 in A, K.488
___ MMO CD 3016 W.A. Mozart Piano Concerto No. 24 in Cm, K.491
___ MMO CD 3017 W.A. Mozart Piano Concerto No. 26 in D, 'Coronation'
___ MMO CD 3018 W.A. Mozart Piano Concerto in G major, K.453
___ MMO CD 3019 Liszt Piano Concerto No. 1/Weber Concertstucke
___ MMO CD 3020 Liszt Piano Concerto No. 2/Hungarian Fantasia
___ MMO CD 3021 J.S. Bach Piano Concerto in Fm/J.C. Bach Concerto in Eb
___ MMO CD 3022 J.S. Bach Piano Concerto in D minor
___ MMO CD 3023 Haydn Piano Concerto in D major
___ MMO CD 3024 Heart Of The Piano Concerto
___ MMO CD 3025 Themes From The Great Piano Concerti
___ MMO CD 3026 Tschiakowsky Piano Concerto No. 1 in Bbm, Opus 23

Music Minus One VOCALIST Compact Discs

___ MMO CD 4001 Schubert Lieder for High Voice
___ MMO CD 4002 Schubert Lieder for Low Voice
___ MMO CD 4003 Schubert Lieder for High Voice   volume 2
___ MMO CD 4004 Schubert Lieder for Low Voice   volume 2
___ MMO CD 4005 Brahms Lieder for High Voice
___ MMO CD 4006 Brahms Lieder for Low Voice
___ MMO CD 4007 Everybody's Favorite Songs for High Voice
___ MMO CD 4008 Everybody's Favorite Songs for Low Voice
___ MMO CD 4009 Everybody's Favorite Songs for High Voice   volume 2
___ MMO CD 4010 Everybody's Favorite Songs for Low Voice   volume 2
___ MMO CD 4011 17th/18th Century Italian Songs High Voice
___ MMO CD 4012 17th/18th Century Italian Songs Low Voice
___ MMO CD 4013 17th/18th Century Italian Songs High Voice   volume 2
___ MMO CD 4014 17th/18th Century Italian Songs Low Voice   volume 2
___ MMO CD 4015 Famous Soprano Arias
___ MMO CD 4016 Famous Mezzo-Soprano Arias
___ MMO CD 4017 Famous Tenor Arias
___ MMO CD 4018 Famous Baritone Arias
___ MMO CD 4019 Famous Bass Arias
___ MMO CD 4020 Hugo Wolf Lieder for High Voice
___ MMO CD 4021 Hugo Wolf Lieder for Low Voice
___ MMO CD 4022 Richard Strauss Lieder for High Voice
___ MMO CD 4023 Richard Strauss Lieder for Low Voice
___ MMO CD 4024 Robert Schumann Lieder for High Voice
___ MMO CD 4025 Robert Schumann Lieder for Low Voice
___ MMO CD 4026 W.A. Mozart Arias For Soprano
___ MMO CD 4027 Verdi Arias For Soprano
___ MMO CD 4028 Italian Arias For Soprano
___ MMO CD 4029 French Arias For Soprano
___ MMO CD 4030 Soprano Oratorio Arias
___ MMO CD 4031 Alto Oratorio Arias
___ MMO CD 4032 Tenor Oratorio Arias
___ MMO CD 4033 Bass Oratorio Arias
___ MMO CD 4041 Beginning Soprano Solos   Kate Hurney, soprano
___ MMO CD 4042 Intermediate Soprano Solos   Kate Hurney, soprano
___ MMO CD 4043 Beginning Mezzo Sop. Solos   Fay Kittelson, mezzo-sop.
___ MMO CD 4044 Intermediate Mezzo-Sop. Solos   Fay Kittelson, mezzo-sop.
___ MMO CD 4045 Advanced Mezzo-Sop. Solos   Fay, Kittelson, mezzo-sop.
___ MMO CD 4046 Beginning Contralto Solos   Carline Ray, mezzo-sop.
___ MMO CD 4047 Beginning Tenor Solos   George Shirley, tenor
___ MMO CD 4048 Intermediate Tenor Solos   George Shirley, tenor
___ MMO CD 4049 Advance Tenor Solos   George Shirley, tenor

Music Minus One FRENCH HORN Compact Discs

___ MMO CD 3501 Mozart: Concerto No. 2, K.417; No. 3, K.447
Choice selections for the French Horn, drawn from the very best solo literature
for the instrument. The pieces are performed by the foremost virtuosi of our
time, artists affiliated with the New York Philharmonic, Boston, Chicago, Cleveland
and Philadelphia Orchestras, The Juilliard School, Curtis Institute of Music,
Indiana University and the Univerity of Toronto, as well as the Metropolitan
Opera Orchestra.

The repertoire and editions used in the Laureate Series correspond to the approved music lists of various Music
Education Associations and may be performed as contest solos in State Music Festivals. Contest regulations, such
as time limitations have been taken into consideration.

Beginning	Intermediate Advanced	Level
___ MMO CD 3502	BAROQUE MUSIC FOR BRASS ENSEMBLE	
___ MMO CD 3511	Mason Jones, Philadelphia Orch.	B
___ MMO CD 3512	Myron Bloom, Cleveland Symphony	B
___ MMO CD 3513	Dale Clevenger, Chicago Symphony	I
___ MMO CD 3514	Mason Jones, Philadelphia Orch.	I
___ MMO CD 3515	Myron Bloom, Cleveland Symphony	A
___ MMO CD 3516	Dale Clevenger, Chicago Symphony	A
___ MMO CD 3517	Mason Jones, Philadelphia Orch.	I
___ MMO CD 3518	Myron Bloom, Cleveland Symphony	A
___ MMO CD 3519	Dale Clevenger, Chicago Symphony	I

Music Minus One VIOLIN Compact Discs

___ MMO CD 3100 Bruch Violin Concerto in Gm
___ MMO CD 3101 Mendelssohn Violin Concerto in Em
___ MMO CD 3102 Tschaikovsky Violin Concerto in D, Opus 35
___ MMO CD 3103 J.S. Bach "Double" Concerto in Dm
___ MMO CD 3104 J.S. Bach Violin Concerti in Am/E
___ MMO CD 3105 J.S. Bach Brandenburg Concerti Nos. 4 and 5
___ MMO CD 3106 J.S. Bach Brandenburg No. 2/Triple Concerto
___ MMO CD 3107 J.S. Bach Concerto in Dm
___ MMO CD 3108 Brahms Violin Concerto in D, Opus 77
___ MMO CD 3109 Chausson Poeme/Schubert Rondo
___ MMO CD 3110 Lalo Symphonie Espagnole
___ MMO CD 3111 Mozart Concerto in D/Vivaldi Concerto in Am
___ MMO CD 3112 Mozart Violin Concerto in A, K.219
___ MMO CD 3113 Wieniawski Concerto in D/Sarasate Zigeunerweisen
___ MMO CD 3114 Viotti Concerto No. 22
___ MMO CD 3115 Beethoven Two Romances/"Spring" Sonata
___ MMO CD 3116 St. Saëns Intro & Rondo Cap./Mozart Serenade & Adagio
___ MMO CD 3117 Beethoven Violin Concerto in D major, Opus 61
___ MMO CD 3118 The Concertmaster Solos from Symphonic Works
___ MMO CD 3119 Air On A G String Favorite Encores for Orchestra
___ MMO CD 3120 Concert Pieces For The Serious Violinist
___ MMO CD 3121 Eighteenth Century Violin Music
___ MMO CD 3122 Violin Favorites With Orchestra Vol. 1 (Easy)
___ MMO CD 3123 Violin Favorites With Orchestra Vol. 2 (Moderate)
___ MMO CD 3124 Violin Favorites With Orchestra Vol. 3 (Mod. Diff.)
___ MMO CD 3125 The Three B's: Bach/Beethoven/Brahms
___ MMO CD 3126 Vivaldi Concerti in Am, D, Am Opus 3 No. 6,9,8
___ MMO CD 3127 Vivaldi "The Four Seasons" 2 CD set $29.98 each
___ MMO CD 3128 Vivaldi "La Tempesta di Mare" Opus 8 No. 5
Albinoni: Violin Concerto in A
___ MMO CD 3129 Vivaldi: Violin Concerto Opus 3 No. 12
Vivaldi Violin Concerto Opus 8, No. 6 "Il Piacere"

Music Minus One CELLO Compact Discs

___ MMO CD 3701 Dvorak: Cello Concerto in B minor, Opus 104
___ MMO CD 3702 C.P.E. Bach: Cello Concerto in A minor
___ MMO CD 3703 Boccherini: Concerto in Bb Major; Bruch: Kol Nidrei

Music Minus One GUITAR Compact Discs

___ MMO CD 3601 Boccherini: Guitar Quintet, No. 4 in D major
___ MMO CD 3602 Giuliani: Guitar Quintet, Opus 65
___ MMO CD 3603 Classic Guitar Duets Easy - Medium

Music Minus One FLUTE Compact Discs

___ MMO CD 3300 Mozart Concerto in D/Quantz Concerto in G
___ MMO CD 3301 Mozart Flute Concerto in G major
___ MMO CD 3302 J.S. Bach Suite No. 2 in Bm
___ MMO CD 3303 Boccherini/Vivaldi Concerti/Mozart Andante
___ MMO CD 3304 Haydn/Vivaldi/Frederick "The Great" Concerti
___ MMO CD 3305 Vivaldi/Telemann/Leclair Flute Concerti
___ MMO CD 3306 J.S. Bach Brandenburg No. 2/Haydn Concerto
___ MMO CD 3307 J.S. Bach Triple Concerto/Vivaldi Concerto No. 9
___ MMO CD 3308 Mozart/Stamitz Flute Quartets
___ MMO CD 3309 Haydn London Trios
___ MMO CD 3310 J.S. Bach Brandenburg Concerti No. 4 and No. 5
___ MMO CD 3311 W.A. Mozart Three Flute Quartets
___ MMO CD 3312 Telemann Am Suite/Gluck 'Orpheus' Scene/Pergolesi Conc. in G
___ MMO CD 3313 Flute Song Easy familiar Classics
___ MMO CD 3314 Vivaldi 3 Flute Concerti RV 427, 438, Opus 10 No. 5
___ MMO CD 3315 Vivaldi 3 Flute Concerti RV 440, Opus 10 No. 4, RV 429
___ MMO CD 3316 Easy Solos, Student Editions, Beginning Level vol. 1
___ MMO CD 3317 Easy Solos, Student Editions, Beginning Level vol. 2
___ MMO CD 3318 Easy Jazz Duets, Student Editions, 1-3 years
Choice selections for the Flute, drawn from the very best solo literature for the
instrument. The pieces are performed by the foremost virtuosi of our time, artists
affiliated with the New York Philharmonic, Boston, Chicago, Cleveland and
Philadelphia Orchestras, The Juilliard School, Curtis Institute of Music, Indiana
University and the Univerity of Toronto, as well as the Metropolitan Opera
Orchestra.

The repertoire and editions used in the Laureate Series correspond to the approved music lists of various Music
Education Associations and may be performed as contest solos in State Music Festivals. Contest regulations, such
as time limitations have been taken into consideration.

Beginning	Intermediate Advanced	Level
___ MMO CD 3321	Murray Pantiz, Philadelphia Orch.	B
___ MMO CD 3322	Donald Peck, Chicago Symphony	B
___ MMO CD 3323	Julius Baker, N.Y. Philharmonic	I
___ MMO CD 3324	Donald Peck, Chicago Symphony	I
___ MMO CD 3325	Murray Panitz, Philadelphia Orch.	A
___ MMO CD 3326	Julius Baker, N.Y. Philharmonic	A
___ MMO CD 3327	Donald Peck, Chicago Symphony	I
___ MMO CD 3328	Murray Panitz, Philadelphia Orch.	A
___ MMO CD 3329	Julius Baker, N.Y. Philharmonic	A
___ MMO CD 3330	Doriot Dwyer, Boston Symphony	B
___ MMO CD 3331	Doriot Dwyer, Boston Symphony	I
___ MMO CD 3332	Doriot Dwyer, Boston Symphony	A

Music Minus One TENOR SAX Compact Discs

___ MMO CD 4201 Easy Tenor Sax Solos, Student Editions, 1-3 years
___ MMO CD 4202 Easy Tenor Sax Solos, Student Editions, 1-3 years
___ MMO CD 4203 Easy Jazz Duets with Rhythm Section, Beginning Level
___ MMO CD 4204 For Saxes Only, Arr. by Bob Wilber

MMO MUSIC GROUP, INC., 50 Executive Boulevard, Elmsford, NY 10523-1325